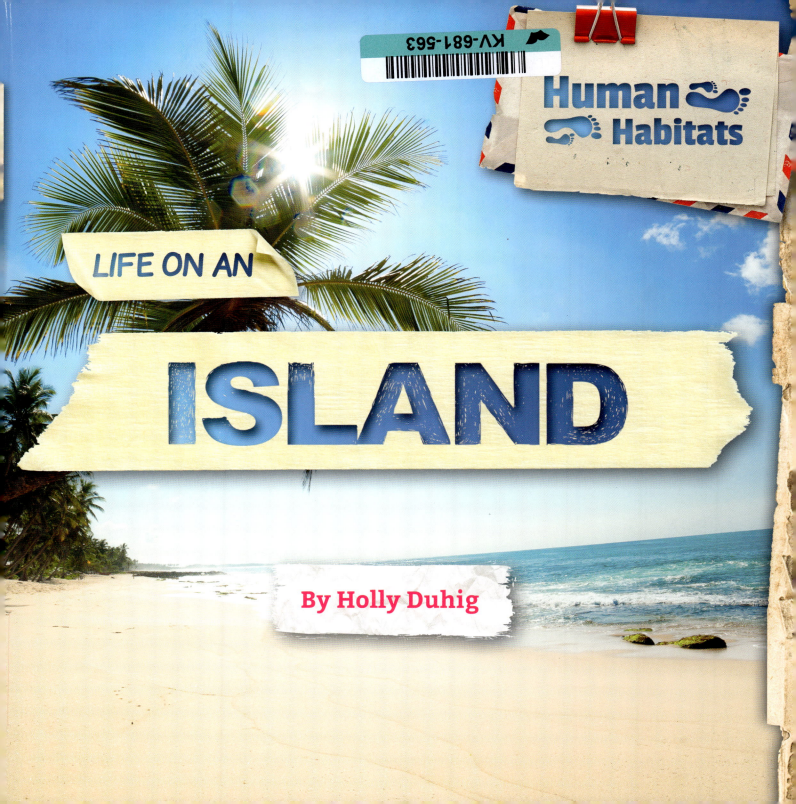

Human Habitats

LIFE ON AN

ISLAND

By Holly Duhig

BookLife
PUBLISHING

©2019
BookLife Publishing Ltd.
King's Lynn
Norfolk PE30 4LS

ISBN: 978-1-78637-587-2

Written by:
Holly Duhig

Edited by:
Emilie Dufresne

Designed by:
Jasmine Pointer

All rights reserved.
Printed in Malaysia.

Photo Credits All images courtesy of Shutterstock. With thanks to Getty Images, Thinkstock Photo and iStockphoto.

Front Cover – Anton Gvozdikov, Deborah Kol, SUPAPORNKH, iShift, 3d_man. Master Images – FARBAI (Germima), givaga, FabrikaSimf (title and label masking tape), andy0man (paper texture), science_photo (petri dish borders) 1 – Anton Gvozdikov. 2 – Anton Gvozdikov. 3 – Deborah Kol. 4 – davegkugler. 5 – Halfpoint, patita haengtham. 6 – Vibrant Image Studioj, YanaKotina. 7 – Ashley Whitworth, BobNoah. 8 & 9 – NAPA. 8 – Naruedom Yaempongsa, boreala. 9 – Patricia Hofmeester, Yevgen Belich. 10 & 11 – aodaodaodaod. 10 – Umomos. 11 – Victor Maschek. 12 & 13 – Standret. 12 – Creative Travel Projects. 13 – Maridav. 14 – Puripat Lertpunyaroj. 15 – Puripat Lertpunyaroj, Nikkytok, kovop58. 16 – Izabela23. 16 & 17 – Alexander Demyanenko. 17 – Shane Myers Photography. 18 & 19 – Ppictures. 18 – Eric Broder Van Dyke. 19 – G Ward Fahey. 20 – Boyan Dimitrov. 21 – MAHATHIR MOHD YASIN, Andrey Solovev. 22 – TSN52. 23 – Pavel Kubarkov, Filip Jedraszak, Baronb, Artem Shadrin, Ruslan Grumble.

CONTENTS

Words that look like **this** can be found in the glossary on page 24.

HUMAN HABITATS

GIRAFFE

A habitat is a place that provides a living thing with food, water and shelter. An animal's body needs to be **adapted** to its habitat. For example, giraffes have long necks for getting food from high up in the trees.

Humans also have habitats. Unlike most animals, humans can survive in many different habitats and our bodies don't need to be adapted to them. Some human habitats are pretty extreme!

Humans don't have long necks; we can just use ladders!

ISLAND HABITATS

Islands are areas of land that are surrounded by water and separated from a **continent**. Some islands make great habitats for humans and animals because they have food, shelter and a good **climate**.

Some islands, such as Ball's Pyramid in the Pacific Ocean, are totally uninhabitable; this means they can't be lived on by humans. Other islands are perfect for living on. For example, Cuba is home to over 11 million people.

BALL'S PYRAMID

CUBA IN THE CARIBBEAN

LIFE IN NEW ZEALAND

AUCKLAND, NEW ZEALAND

NORTH ISLAND

SOUTH ISLAND

New Zealand

New Zealand is a country made up of two main islands – North Island and South Island – with around 600 smaller islands surrounding them. New Zealand is home to people from many different **cultures**.

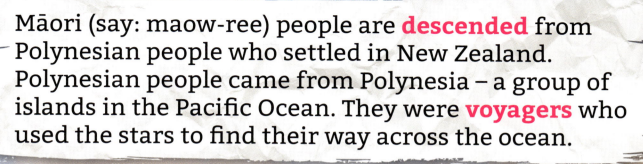

Māori (say: maow-ree) people are **descended** from Polynesian people who settled in New Zealand. Polynesian people came from Polynesia – a group of islands in the Pacific Ocean. They were **voyagers** who used the stars to find their way across the ocean.

MĀORI CANOES

Traditional
MĀORI GREETING

KAITIAKITANGA

Māori people in traditional clothing.

Māori people have their own language called Te Reo. The word 'kaitiakitanga' in this language means to respect and look after the **natural environment**. Looking after the environment means not taking too many things from nature.

To look after the environment, Māori people made rules about how much fishing people were allowed to do. This helped to keep rivers and lakes in New Zealand healthy and full of fish.

It is important to them to look after the māuri – life force – of the forest.

LIFE IN ICELAND

ICELAND

Iceland is an island country that is very far north. This means it has a very cold climate. Very cold islands don't usually make very good human habitats, but Iceland is different.

Iceland has many volcanoes. The underground **magma** that forms these volcanoes helps to heat water underground. This is called geothermal (say: jee-oh-ther-mal) heating and it creates hot springs all over the country.

HOT SPRING, ICELAND

HOT SPRINGS

BLUE LAGOON HOT SPRING POOL, ICELAND

Natural hot springs can be extremely hot and very dangerous, but some are the perfect temperature to bathe in. The Blue Lagoon is very popular with local people and **tourists**.

Icelandic people use geothermally-heated water in their homes for things such as washing, cooking and heating. It is also used in swimming pools! Using naturally heated water is very good for the environment.

LIFE IN HAWAII

HONOLULU, HAWAII'S CAPITAL CITY

Hawaii is a group of islands that can be found far out in the Pacific Ocean. These islands are part of the United States of America, but they still have their own culture.

Like New Zealand, Hawaii was first found and settled by Polynesians. The islands were not the perfect human habitat to begin with because there were hardly any plants that produced food for humans.

MAKING A PARADISE

POI

Poi is a traditional Hawaiian food made using the underground stem of the taro plant.

The Polynesians brought many different plants and crops to Hawaii, so they would have food to eat. They also brought pigs and chickens. Over time, the Polynesians turned Hawaii into the perfect human paradise!

Hawaii is well known for a traditional form of dance called the hula dance. Hula dancing became very popular in America so now there are two types of hula dancing: hula 'auana and hula kahiko. Hula kahiko is the traditional Polynesian dancing.

HULA KAHIKO DANCE

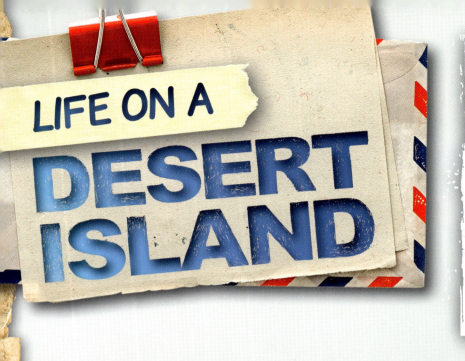

LIFE ON A DESERT ISLAND

A desert island is an island that nobody lives on. You may have heard stories of brave explorers being **marooned** on desert islands and having to learn how to survive. Many of these stories are based on real desert island castaways.

ALEXANDER SELKIRK

Alexander Selkirk was the **inspiration** for Daniel Defoe's Robinson Crusoe.

Robinson Crusoe

Alexander Selkirk was a Scottish sailor who was a castaway on a desert island for four years. Alexander survived by eating shellfish, fish and wild goats. The goats also gave him milk.

MARGUERITE DE LA ROCQUE

Marguerite de La Rocque was marooned on the Isle of Demons by her uncle for falling in love with a young man. She survived by living in a cave and hunting wild animals.

She was marooned with the man and her maidservant but they both died.

ACTIVITY

If you were marooned
on a desert island,
what five things would
you take with you
to help you survive?

GLOSSARY

ADAPTED	changed over time to suit the environment
CLIMATE	the common weather in a certain place
CONTINENT	a large area of land that is made up of many countries
CULTURES	the traditions, ideas and ways of life of groups of people
DESCENDED	to have come from and be related to a specific person or group
INSPIRATION	to be influenced by someone or something
MAGMA	molten, liquid rock below or within the Earth's crust
MAROONED	to be left on an island or coastline without a way to get off
NATURAL ENVIRONMENT	the animals, plants and natural features that make up a certain place
TOURISTS	people who visit a place for pleasure
TRADITIONAL	related to very old behaviours or beliefs
VOYAGERS	people who take long trips by air, land or sea, or into space

INDEX